SCOTLAND'S
WICKED
WITCHES

CHARLES SINCLAIR

GOBLINSHEAD
COCKENZIE HOUSE

First published 2011, Reprinted 2017
© Martin Coventry & Joyce Miller 2011

Published by
GOBLINSHEAD
Cockenzie House, 22 Edinburgh Road
Cockenzie EH32 0SZ, Scotland
www.goblinshead.co.uk

British Library Cataloguing in Publication Data
A catalogue record for this book is available from
the British Library.

ISBN 978 1899874 53 8

Typeset by GOBLINSHEAD
Printed and bound in Glasgow, Scotland, by Bell & Bain

Disclaimer:
The information contained in this *Scotland's Wicked Witches* (the
"Material") is believed to be accurate at the time of printing, but no
representation or warranty is given (express or implied) as to its
accuracy, completeness or correctness. The author and publisher do not
accept any liability whatsoever for any direct, indirect or consequential
loss or damage arising in any way from any use of or reliance on this
Material for any purpose.

While every care has been taken to compile and check all the
information in this book, it is possible that mistakes may have occurred.
If you know of any corrections, alterations or improvements, please
contact the author or the publishers at the address above.

Contents

Introduction

This book is about wicked witches, or more correctly about people who were accused by their peers of being wicked witches. Whether they were, of course, is now impossible to determine. But from the end of the sixteenth century until well into the eighteenth century such a determination of innocence or guilt was a matter of life or death, indeed a very public death that involved strangulation and then the bodily remains being burnt. And that this was taken seriously by all parts of Scottish society is clearly evident as around 4,000 people were accused of witchcraft, sorcery and malefice (harmful magic) during this period.

But why was witchcraft and magic so important? Why were so many obsessed by the Devil and his servants?

Some of the answer lies in the times from which the witchcraft hunts come. Scottish society underwent unprecedented change from the Reformation in Scotland in the 1560s right through to the Jacobite Risings of the early eighteenth century. This was a time of uncertainty and fear. Nothing was set any more. The Catholic church had been thrown out of Scotland but the new reorganised form of Christianity had yet to be decided. Religious practices changed radically. No longer were idolatrous images or ornamentation or festivals to be tolerated. A Bible in English would be published. Rituals that society had relied on were now banned, such as visiting saints' relics or holy wells for healing or good luck. It was a pious time when strict adherence to the reformed faith was required, and power devolved from bishops to ministers with increased personal responsibility for sanctity among the ordinary folk. It should be emphasised that most people truly believed in good and in evil, and in their representatives – in Christ and in God, but also in the Devil and in demons.

This was also a time of great social change. Not even monarchs were safe. Mary, Queen of Scots, was forced from the throne of Scotland and was eventually executed by Elizabeth of England. Her son, James VI, united the thrones of Scotland and England. Yet after a horrific and protracted civil war that engulfed the whole of Britain, Charles I (James VI's son) was beheaded and Oliver Cromwell became Lord Protector. His troops occupied Scotland after more bloodshed. His regime fell with the execution of his son and the Restoration of Charles II in 1660. But then James VII of Scotland and II of England 'abdicated' his throne and fled Britain in 1689, and so began fifty years of Jacobite Risings. The whole period is peppered with conflict, at international, national and local level.

Life was also hard for ordinary people. Warfare crippled the economy and took men from the fields. Periods of terrible weather caused crops to fail and regular famines. Plague and pestilence, the Black Death, ravaged many places.

All this put the society of the time under extreme pressure, out of which burst the witch hunts.

It is clear that society in general believed in what might be called magic; that is a ritual with objects and words (a spell, in other words) to manipulate the world to achieve a desired outcome. This could, of course, benefit society by providing healing, fortune-telling, love potions, finding lost or stolen goods, and protective or good-luck charms. This might be called white magic, and the practitioners of it were known as charmers in Scotland. Indeed it was believed that illness was caused by malign spirits that could be removed by transference, giving the illness to another creature, object or even to another person.

But in a society that believed in evil and in the Devil, a practitioner of white magic might just as easily and quickly turn their powers on someone they did not like or with whom they had argued. After all, they had the power to cause illness as well as to remove it, to steal crops and drink by diabolic means, cause storms, seduce the unwary, even kill using elf shot or fairy darts (now known to be prehistoric arrow heads) or making a wax or butter effigy. In all likelihood not only did the victims believe in witchcraft but so also did those accused. Indeed some of the accused may well have actually believed that they had at least some magical powers, whatever the source, and – who knows – maybe they truly did

This belief might have been enough for the local population to accuse someone of witchcraft but the authorities, such as the government, judiciary and Privy Council, needed more. They required a diabolic pact, where the witch renounced her baptism in a Satanic ceremony, an inversion of the Christian service. These witches would fornicate with the Devil, gather themselves into groups or covens for outrageous parties, cast spells to harm their contemporaries, even try to sink the ships on which James VI and his new bride Anne of Denmark were returning to Scotland. Commissions were issued by the authorities so that investigations could be held, although many took matters into their own hands.

In the sixteenth century, excruciating torture was permissible as a way of gaining a confession, so it is perhaps not surprising that so many people confessed to accusations of malefice and diabolic pact, even if many then later retracted their confessions. As the seventeenth century progressed, torture was no longer sanctioned by the central authorities, although sleep deprivation and starvation were still widely used. The number of prosecutions did not diminish, however, until the end of that century.

It is certainly true that the weight of evidence needed to prosecute people on such a serious charge seem inconceivable now. Accusers could be part of the juries, witnesses could use hearsay with no corroborating evidence. The result was, of course, that disputes and name-calling could escalate and those individuals who were unpopular could be targeted with little to save them if their contemporaries were willing to testify against them.

Most of those charged were women, older in age, single or widowed, of the lower order. It is worth mentioning, however, most were accused by their own neighbours of similar status. There were some cases where burgesses and even nobles were charged, although behind these were usually either a property or a financial or a political motive.

There were also at least three episodes of demonic possession, not dissimilar to the Salem case in the USA, when teenagers denounced people around them. That these may have been encouraged by ministers of the church is certainly possible. By the turn of the eighteenth century, the thirst for witch hunting was diminishing, partly due to a growing rationalism in society, while a new wording of the Witchcraft Act in 1737 finally stopped the prosecutions.

Records for this period are far from complete. Some cases have contemporary accounts, such as the North Berwick witch trials, although the veracity of some of these cannot be determined. Kirk session records and state papers also survive and provide much valuable information.

But in many cases little or nothing remains, until it is difficult to be certain that even 'well-known' witches, such as Maggie Wall, Kate MacNiven or Janet Horne, ever existed.

In the end, of course, that does not really matter. They still commemorate the many hundreds – possibly thousands – of women (and men) who were found guilty of being wicked witches and who were then publicly executed by being throttled and having their bodies consumed by fire.

Charles Sinclair
May 2011

Janet Douglas
1537

The story of Janet Douglas, Lady Glamis, is a tragic tale of vengeance against an innocent young woman, meted out by the king of the time, James V, and achieved by accusing her on a baseless charge of witchcraft and poisoning.

Janet was the daughter of George Douglas, Master of Angus (heir, at that time, to the Earldom of Angus) and Elizabeth Drummond, daughter of the first Lord Drummond, and was born around 1505. She married John Lyon, sixth Lord Glamis, and they had a son, who they also called John. When Lyon died in 1528, the young widowed Janet went on to wed Walter Campbell of Skipness. Janet was also the sister of Archibald Douglas, sixth Earl of Angus, and it was this family relationship that was to be her downfall.

So why did James hates the Douglases? James V was just a child when his father, James IV, was slain with the flower of Scottish nobility at the disastrous Battle of Flodden in 1513. James IV's widow, Margaret Tudor, went on to marry the Douglas Earl of Angus and, as stepfather to the young king, Angus virtually controlled the kingdom by having possession of the king. When James V came of age, he escaped from Falkland Palace and Angus's clutches and asserted his power. Angus fled Scotland after being besieged in Tantallon Castle in

1528, but James went on to pursue vengeance against his family. Janet was widowed the same year that her brother fled Scotland; James had forfeited the Earl of Angus, seizing his lands and property.

Janet was summoned on a charge of communicating with her exiled brother, but she failed to appear and was then forfeited herself. She and her family were besieged in Glamis Castle and then seized and brought to Edinburgh. Although a women of impeccable character, she was accused of trying to poison James and also of witchcraft, although it took torturing Janet's servants and friends to find any evidence against her on these charges (she may well have been guilty on the original charge).

She was imprisoned with her husband Walter Campbell and her son John in a dark dungeon of Edinburgh Castle. Although nearly blind from her jail, Janet made an eloquent speech in her defence at her trial, but it was to no avail and she was convicted, along with her son. Campbell managed to escape from the prison but he was killed, falling from the castle rock.

Unfortunately nothing could save Janet and on 17 July 1537, on what is now the esplanade of Edinburgh Castle, she was burned alive; her son was forced to watch. She was described as 'in the prime of her years, of a singular beauty, and suffering through all, though a woman, with a man-like courage'.

John, her son, was also sentenced to death but, fortunately for him, he was not yet of an age when

Glamis Castle, home to Janet Douglas, Lady Glamis.

he could be executed; that was reserved for when he reached eighteen. In the meantime, James V took all his lands and houses, including Glamis Castle, and plundered them. Luckily for John, James died in 1542 before he could be executed, and John was subsequently pardoned and became seventh Lord Glamis and recovered his property.

Glamis Castle is said to be haunted by the ghost of Janet Douglas, an apparition known as the Grey Lady, and reputedly seen on many occasions in the chapel of the old stronghold. One occasion was reported in 1716 during the visit of James, the Old Pretender, during the Jacobite Rising, when her ghost was seen praying at one of the pews. This James was, of course, the direct descendant of the man who had sent her to her death.

Alison Pearson
1588

This is an interesting early case from 1588 – before the major and notorious episode of witchcraft trials at North Berwick. Alison Pearson – Alesoun Pierson in the original records was from Byrehills (or Boarhills) in Fife, three miles south of St Andrews. The details of her accusation and confession are memorable as, although there are the usual mentions of the Devil and malefice, Alison claimed the devil-figure was in fact her cousin or uncle, Mr William Sympsoun or Simpson. She also described in detail her association and travels with the 'Court of Elfame' or the elves or fairies. Alison also appears to have been involved in healing – and a particularly high status individual, the Archbishop of St Andrews, Patrick Adamson – although ultimately the 'cure' was unsuccessful. This latter act did not do Alison any favours, as it was interpreted as malefice and contributed to her conviction.

Alison had been in trouble before 1588. Five years earlier it appears that she was in custody under suspicion of being a witch and at this point Patrick Adamson, the Archbishop, was involved. Adamson was not a very well-regarded person within the kirk in Scotland. Although Scotland was nominally presbyterian at this time, there was tension between the kirk and the king, James VI, who would the following year, 1584, reintroduce an episcopal church

St Andrews Castle, the palace of the Archbishops of St Andrews.

government. Adamson was keen to gain favour with the king and supported James's episcopalian proposals. By 1586 he was so out of favour with other ministers that he was excommunicated (thrown out of the church) – quite an achievement given that, next to the king, he was theoretically the most powerful churchman in the country.

During earlier years 1582-3, however, he had been quite unwell – some claimed as a result of a curse by the widow of a man who had been tricked out of property by the Archbishop. It seems that Adamson turned to witchcraft and witches to procure a cure. Once the kirk session got wind of this, Adamson was himself called before them to answer accusations about believing in and using witchcraft. Alison, who by 1588, might have been around forty-one years old, was accused of sorcery and 'invocation of spirits of the Devil, especially in the vision and form of Mr William Sympsoun, her cousin' – sometimes he was referred to as her uncle, so the exact relationship is not clear, but he appears to have been only six or so years older than her. According to Alison's account, she had been sent to live with him in Edinburgh when she was twelve years old to be treated for an illness. She claimed that Simpson was a learned man, a scholar, who had medical knowledge.

Again it is difficult to explain exactly what 'learning' Simpson had as his own background is also shrouded with somewhat unusual events. According to some sources, it was reported that he had been stolen by an Egyptian giant when he was only a boy. There is of course a different way to explain this event as, at this time, the sixteenth century, 'Egyptian' was the term for gypsy, people who were not well liked by the state and who were the object of official legislation limiting their movements and behaviours. So one interpretation might be that Simpson was whisked off to the exotic and mysterious East where he learnt medical and other mystical skills – maybe even the Black Arts. Or, more prosaically, he moved around the country with a group of travelling people learning their traditions and customs.

This account has Simpson as a flesh and blood mortal person with a history, but another reading of Alison's testimony might be that he may have been a spirit or ghost: the distinction is not always clear.

Simpson in this latter form is relevant as Alison gave detailed descriptions of his relationship with the fairies or elves, whose company she also kept for several years. She said that she saw Simpson with the 'good neighbours', as the elves were also known, but it is not clear if Simpson introduced her to the fairies as he was with them as the spirit of a deceased person – perhaps as a form of spirit guide for Alison – or if he was able to cross the boundary between the realms of humans and spirits – into Middle Earth – as a mortal being like Alison. It was said that Simpson could predict the arrival of the fairies by the sound of a whirl wind, so it does seem as if he was her intermediary between the two realms.

Alison described the court of Elfame in detail: she met the queen and men in green. Indeed a man in green approached her and offered her rewards if she would be his servant. Alison claimed she cried out God's name and rejected this offer and the man in green left: it would seem likely that this could have been interpreted by the authorities in 1588 as a form of demonic pact. Presumably in an attempt at defence of any accusation of being the devil's servant, Alison mentioned rejecting similar offers on more than one occasion, by crossing herself or saying a prayer.

The fairies not only had a queen and court, but enjoyed music and laughter, dancing and singing, food and drink. Although it seems that she had returned to Boarhills after her treatment in Edinburgh, Alison described meeting the fairies –

or being transported by the fairies – at various places: Grangemuir, St Andrews and Edinburgh. One account has her spirited off to fairyland for seven years, the standard length of visit to the spirit realm although this seems a little too conveniently poetic, as in the case of True Thomas, also known as Thomas the Rhymer.

Despite the festive frolics of these meetings, Alison's version also implied that she was quite frightened of the fairies and their powers, although they showed her how to make salves and potions using herbs and other ingredients which benefited her. She was shown when to gather the plants – before sunrise – and how to boil and distil them into magical medicines. Of course the other source of this knowledge Alison claimed was Simpson himself. Nevertheless, despite these seeming rewards the fairies also punished Alison frequently by hurting her side.

It does though seem that however Alison had gained her healing knowledge, she used her skills and was consulted by local people from the St Andrews area for several years. This appears to be how the connection with Archbishop Adamson developed. It seems he suffered from numerous complaints – fevers, heart problems, and general weakness, and sought help from several different healers. Her treatments included: herbs in claret, yew's milk and boiled chicken, and also a salve which was rubbed on several areas of his body; hardly very 'magical' it would appear.

The jury found her guilty and she was

executed probably by the standard means: strangled and then burned. Adamson himself died a few years later in 1592 not, apparently due to any devilish or magical means, but certainly in much reduced circumstances. Having been deprived of office in 1579, then excommunicated, and, finally, to have admitted consulting witches, he lost his position and influence over national church, and political, affairs.

Katherine Ross and Hector Munro 1590

On 22nd July 1590 Katherine Ross, Lady Foulis, and her stepson Hector Munro, were tried for attempted murder and magic. Katherine was the second wife of Robert Munro, the fifteenth Baron of Foulis. He had two sons – Robert and Hector – and three daughters from his first marriage, and a further three sons and four daughters with Katherine.

This case involves accusations of the consultation and use of malicious witchcraft in order to cause the death of Robert, Katherine's stepson. It is a complicated case but in many ways the attempted murder was not so very unusual for sixteenth-century Scotland. There were many murders or attempted murders, throughout Scottish history, particularly of people with property and status. These could often result in convoluted plots involving more than one person and secret bonds and alliances. There have been imprisonments resulting in starvation, poisoning, burning, stabbing, and some which required a combination of these methods. Most of these murders were for gain or for revenge, were often the result of jealousy and were cold blooded and premeditated. Many accusations of witchcraft that were made about individuals often had an element of high emotion on both sides, both accuser and accused. Anger, jealousy, revenge contributing to disputes and verbal exchanges, but cases like Lady Foulis and Hector Munro – and the Erskines of Dun (also in this book) – were much more to do with greed and ambition. Although emotions may have been running high, these plots were planned. They were less about the Devil and supernatural powers and more about straightforward, murder.

Robert Munro was heir to the barony title and property, and Katherine plotted with his brother Hector to murder Robert, so that Hector could inherit. Another part of her plan was to murder Marjory Campbell, the wife of her brother George Ross. George was the laird of Balnagowan and he could then marry Robert Munro's widow, who it seems must have been quite wealthy. It is likely that her brother George Ross knew about the plans, but he was not charged as an accomplice. It all sounds like the plot for a particularly gruesome soap opera!

Although the trial was in 1590, the events themselves occurred as early as 1576-77. The accusations included witchcraft, sorcery, incantation and poisoning. Although ultimately poisoning would seem to have been the most effective method, the plotters also used a range of magical rituals to cause malefice and also consulted a number of other people for advice about magic and used servants to deliver packages or food to their intended victims. Widening the plot in part contributed to Katherine and Hector's demise as much of the evidence against them came from the confessions made by these other people.

Balnagowan Castle, Katherine Ross's family home.

In 1576, Katherine sent a witch, Agnes Roy, to another witch who was known as Laskie Loncart in order to discover if her plots against Robert and Marjory would be successful. Loncart seemingly recommended that Katherine should go to the Hill of Nigg and there meet with the fairies who would advise her. In September of that year and the following Easter, she paid William MacGillivray with linen and money to procure for her some unknown magical items. At the same time MacGillivray bought rat poison.

The first attempts to kill Robert and Marjory involved magic and witchcraft, and featured a number of malicious rituals that were commonly associated with demonic witchcraft. After Easter of 1577, Katherine purchased a number of specific magical items, including a fairy dart or elf shot, which cost four shillings. The next stage involved the use of image magic and would have included hair or some other personal item from the intended victim. She and three accomplices, including Loncart, made an image or representation of Robert from butter, which was then shot at with the fairy dart. The attempt to hit the butter image failed and so shortly after another figure was made, this time from clay. Once again the image was not hit by the dart.

Nevertheless a further failed attempt to use image magic was carried out in the summer of 1577. By this time Katherine had consulted a further two people, Christian Ross and Thomas MacKane, and it seems she specifically requested MacKane to murder her sister-in-law using magic, for which task he would be financially rewarded. It is not clear if MacKane tried anything but Marjory was still alive by the end of the summer.

The next attempt was to take place on All Hallows Eve – 31 October – when both image magic and poison would be used. A poisoned drink was to be delivered to Robert, and Katherine (once again) got Loncart to shoot at clay images of both Robert and Marjory with fairy darts.

Although Katherine appears to have concentrated on using image magic, despite its recurrent failure, she also resorted to the use of poison on a number of occasions, which were also equally as unsuccessful. On one such, rather than the intended victims a servant or nurse tasted the poisoned food first and subsequently died. Another attempt nearly cost the lives of the wider extended family, including her erstwhile accomplice Hector and his children. It seems that the poison was spilt so it did not find its way into the meal. Marjory Campbell was alleged to have eaten poisoned meat, but again did not die. Luck seems to have been with the intended victims on more than one occasion. Or perhaps Katherine and her accomplices were simply incompetent.

Katherine's husband Robert who, up to this point, appears to have either been in ignorance or had turned a blind eye then took an active role and in late 1577 obtained a commission to investigate accusations about the use of magic, incantation, and murder in the area. The people named in the commission included many of those whom Katherine had consulted. Some of them were burned before the end of year but others managed to evade arrest temporarily.

A further commission was issued in January 1578 when more people were arrested, tried and convicted, including William MacGillivray. Thomas MacKane was burned in Dingwall later in 1578. Katherine's brother George was questioned about events and Katherine made a declaration that she was willing to be tried for witchcraft but that she was innocent of the charges. She then sought shelter and protection from her uncle, the Earl of Caithness, for the next nine months or so.

Robert the younger inherited the title in 1588 and in 1589 he applied for a commission to try suspected witches. Wider events then intervened and there was a bit of trouble amongst the northern nobility, some of whom were still Catholic. James VI was informed that they had been in communication with Catholic Spain and despite an attempt to oppose the king led by the Earl of Huntly, James succeeded in quashing any rebellion in the bud. As a result of the upheaval Katherine managed to persuade the king to suspend Robert's commission.

It was, however, only a postponement and in July 1590 she attended court accused of a litany of crimes, all of which she denied. Many of the witnesses did not turn up and the jury, which was comprised of fifteen men, from her local area of Cromarty, Tain and Dingwall, acquitted her on all charges. The jury was carefully selected; they were her social inferiors and they all had a connection to the family and so could be persuaded to give a favourable verdict.

The person who led the prosecution case against her was, interestingly, her other stepson Hector who had been her erstwhile accomplice; his own trial for similar charges was on the same day. Katherine claimed that Hector had deliberately obtained a commission so that he could arrest and try her innocent servants. Throughout the months prior to the trials, Katherine and Hector submitted claims and counterclaims against each other about harassment, money and indemnity. Both trials were delayed as a result but were eventually held in July.

Hector was accused on three counts of using magic and witchcraft, but ironically it would seem that in 1588 Hector claimed he sent for witches to help cure his brother Robert's illness. It is not clear whether Robert himself knew that he was being treated using magic, but it was reported that they used some of his hair and nail cuttings in order to 'diagnose' the prognosis of the condition. It should be noted, however, that hair and nails were also often used in malicious rituals to inflict harm, so there would seem to have been a bit of ambivalence or fudging perhaps? Robert did not die of the illness and inherited the title that year.

Another incident the following year involved Hector himself being treated for an illness by a charmer using three magical stones which, it was claimed, produced water. According to contemporary cultural explanations about causes and cures for illnesses, Hector's illness would have to be transferred to someone else if he was to get better, and the person targeted was Hector's half-brother George, Katherine's eldest son. Hector may also have had a sexual liaison with Marion MacIngaroch, the charmer, as they seem to have been in each other's company between January 1589 until just before his trial the following year. Hector did recover from his complaint and in April 1590 George Munro took ill and died. It was on this count of murder that Hector was charged and tried, but like his stepmother, Hector's jury was made up of local men, some of whom had been on Katherine's jury, and Hector was found not guilty on all three charges.

North Berwick
Witch Trials
1590

One of the most famous, notorious and complicated witchcraft accusations are those of North Berwick. North Berwick is a pleasant seaside town on the south coast of the Firth of Forth in East Lothian in the south-east of Scotland. The main incident reportedly took place among the ruins of the old parish church by the shore, a part of which can still be visited on the way to the Seabird Centre (the church was a ruin even at the time of the trial, having been partly washed away in a storm).

This episode involved members of society from the lowest to the highest, from the king of the

Old parish church, North Berwick.

time, James VI, to maidservants, and many in between: peasants, the wives of advocates and Edinburgh burgesses, and finally a Scottish Earl. Although quite early in the cycle of witchcraft trials, it involves many elements that were to appear repeatedly in later accusations and James VI wrote his influential work *Daemonologie* based on this episode and a similar case in Denmark.

GEILLIS DUNCAN

Geillis (or Gelie in documents) Duncan was a maidservant in the service of David Seaton, who was a baillie depute in the East Lothian village of Tranent. Seaton had become aware that Geillis was often absent from his house without explanation during the night and became suspicious of her behaviour; he confronted her and then interrogated her. Why he thought she might be involved in witchcraft, and not just fornication or adultery, is not clear, although it may have been because Geillis had a reputation as a charmer: a wise woman or healer. Seaton would have, of course, as a churchgoer, been aware of concerns about malefice and witchcraft during the turbulent period when the reformed church was being established in Scotland after 1560.

Whatever the cause, Seaton had Geillis arrested and she was imprisoned in the tolbooth of Haddington, although he had not sought permission from the authorities. Geillis denied any wrongdoing. Poor Geillis was then tortured – a not uncommon method for extracting a confession in the sixteenth century – and pilliwinks were used on her, crushing her fingers, and she was also tortured by 'binding or winching her head with a cord or rope'. Seaton also had her body searched for a Devil's mark by a local pricker, looking for a blemish on her skin where she felt no pain, and such a mark was found on her neck.

Perhaps, not surprisingly, Geillis then confessed; a long and detailed testimony. She told them she had made a pact with the Devil, and that she had attended meetings with other witches at several places, of which the old kirk of North Berwick was one. Those she implicated included Agnes Sampson from Haddington, Bessie Thomson from Edinburgh, Dr John Fian from Prestonpans, Janet Stratton, Donald Robson, Ritchie Graham, as well as Euphame MacCalzean and Barbara Napier, both of whom were well-to-do ladies from Edinburgh. These two were related to Thomas MacCalzean, Lord Cliftonhall, Provost of Edinburgh and Senator of the College of Justice. Indeed, Euphame was his daughter and heir, yet despite her high status, she was to suffer a most horrible death.

Geillis was held from December 1590 until June 1591 and was repeatedly questioned before finally being executed by being strangled and burned. Before she died, however, she claimed that all the things she had said about her co-accused were lies; this was however too late to influence their fate. Bessie Thomson was also executed.

JOHN FIAN

John Fian from Prestonpans, also in East Lothian, was also soon in custody, having been arrested in December 1590, although he was to die quite soon after, in late January of the following year. Much of the information about John Fian and his co-accused comes from a pamphlet called 'Newes from Scotland', which was published in London in 1591 and claimed to detail the 'damnable life of Doctor

'Newes from Scotland', 1591.

Fian, a notable sorcerer, who was burned at Edenbrough in January last'. The author remained anonymous, although was most likely at least present at the trials, but it seems likely the accounts were heavily edited and sensationalised to make the pamphlet more saleable. Indeed, the veracity of the document may be questioned at many points.

Dr John Fian appears to have been a character of some note: among his many other claimed misdemeanours was a confession that he had committed fornication with some thirty-two different women. He also had a number of aliases, such as John Fean, John Cunningham, John Sibbet and, of course, Dr Fian. Fian was the schoolmaster at Prestonpans, although he also taught in nearby Tranent, where he may have first come into contact with Geillis Duncan. Like Geillis, Fian was tortured before he confessed by being partially throttled and later, when he refused to co-operate further, his feet and legs were crushed by the use of the boot. Fian repented and escaped from prison but he was recaptured and mistreated further, by having his fingernails ripped out and nails hammered into the tips of his fingers. Before his execution, Fian retracted his confessions, claiming – quite reasonably – they had been extracted by torture. It made no difference, of course, and he was strangled and burned, also on Castle Hill in Edinburgh.

One of the most absurd tales, which would be comic if the circumstances surrounding it were not so terrible, was a spell Fian was supposed to have cast that went badly wrong. Fian desired the sister of one of his students and tried to use love magic to attract her. To do this, however, he needed hairs from the object of his fancy and he asked the lady's brother to procure these for him. The student, however, believing something was amiss, went to his mother with the request and the mother substituted three hairs from the udder of a cow. Fian worked his spell using the hairs and was then chased around by the love struck cow.

More seriously Fian also confessed that he was present at all the witches' meetings, including at

North Berwick, when the Devil was always present. As a literate man, he was the 'clerk' and took the diabolic oaths of true service to the Devil from those present. He also described how candles, sermons, prayers and preaching were all used in a Satanic inversion of the Christian service. The group had, among other things, ruined crops, destroyed livestock, killed men and caused storms, including one intended to drown James VI and Anne of Denmark when they returned to Scotland. This latter action was of course, one of treason, although he later went back on this confession.

AGNES SAMPSON

A third accused was the widow Agnes Sampson (or Sampsoune), who was from the hamlet of Nether Keith, by the grand mansion of Keith Marischal, near the village of Humbie in East Lothian. In 1589 she was questioned by the Haddington synod, but from the turn of the following year she was interrogated by no less a person than James VI at Holyrood Palace in Edinburgh. His interest may have been partly fuelled by a case in Denmark the previous year, when six women were accused of witchcraft and trying to prevent Anne, James's wife, from reaching Scotland. Initially, Agnes refused to confess but, like the others, she was tortured and searched by a witch pricker, and went on to name others she claimed were involved: Katharine Gray, David Steel and Janet Campbell, as well as Barbara Napier and Euphame MacCalzean; in the end fifty-nine other people were named. Indeed, she went on to tell the king that more than two-hundred witches were involved. Her crimes, she said, included attending covens and sabbats, using magical charms, and being involved in trying to murder the king and his bride.

Like Geillis Duncan, Agnes was known as a healer, or a charmer as it was called in Scotland, and her clients included both the poor and ordinary folk and lords, lairds and their womenfolk, from places such as North Berwick, Dirleton, Preston(pans) and Dalkeith. As well as attempting to cure illnesses (although not always successfully), she also helped reduced the pain of childbirth. Agnes was paid for her work and claimed that she had learned what she knew from her father. Initially, Agnes only acknowledged her healing and charming, such as divination and love magic, rejecting the Satanic nature of her work, but over the course of a week she confessed to witchcraft. It is entirely possible that she was tortured during this time...

After her husband had died, she claimed that the Devil had come to her, and she had followed him because of poverty and revenge. A Devil's mark was found on her right knee, although she said that she had thought that the injured spot had been received from one of her children while they were in bed. She claimed that she invoked the Devil when healing folk, called him 'Elva' or 'Eloa', and he appeared to her in the form of a dog.

Agnes described, in colourful if not entirely credible detail, how on Halloween (All Hallow's Eve or the 31 October) of 1590, some two-hundred witches had journeyed across the sea by sieve to the

Witches dining at the witches' sabbat.

old kirk at North Berwick, bringing fine wine and ale with them. Here they met the Devil and there was a huge party with singing and dancing – indeed, she claimed that Geillis Duncan had played on a Jew's Harp (a small musical instrument held between the teeth and plucked with the finger). She also said that the witches all had to kiss the Devil's bottom, and they performed an inversion of the Christian service, with prayers and black candles.

At the ceremony, one of eleven that she described, the Devil had baptised a cat, which he then threw into the sea. This spell was to raise a storm with which to sink the ships conveying James VI and Anne of Denmark back to Scotland, the Devil saying, 'the king is the greatest enemy he has in the world' (according to 'Newes from Scotland'). James had indeed come through rough weather, although this was hardly unusual in the North Sea at the end of October. His ship survived the voyage but a sister

Bass Rock from the old parish church, North Berwick.

vessel, carrying his new queen's treasure and valuables, was lost.

Up to this point it is thought that James had actually remained somewhat sceptical, even saying (again from 'Newes from Scotland'), 'they [the accused] were all extreme liars'. Agnes then apparently took James aside and whispered in his ear the exact words that passed between James and Anne on their wedding night. This is an interesting admission by her, not least that it would almost certainly get her executed…

Her confession did not stop there. She described how they used wax figures and animals, and invoked a spirit in the form of a white stag. One spell included collecting the venom from a toad, which had also been intended to harm the king, although she also needed to use an item of the king's clothing or something he owned. Apparently one of the king's servants, John Kers, was asked to help them but, perhaps luckily for the king, he refused. She also claimed that she used parts of corpses in her spells.

When the unfortunate Agnes had no more to confess, on 28 January 1591 she was strangled and then burnt. At the end, it is said she was penitent and prayed to God for salvation.

BARBARA NAPIER

As mentioned before, Barbara Napier and Euphame MacCalzean were implicated by others, although their part should have been minor. Barbara Napier was married to Archibald Douglas and her brother was a rich Edinburgh burgess so she was wealthy enough to employ a defence counsel.

The accusations against her were principally that she had consulted witches, not that she was a witch herself, and had used the services of Agnes Sampson and Ritchie Graham. She had procured the assistance and advice of Agnes to help Jean Lyon, wife of the eighth Earl of Angus, who was suffering vomiting during her pregnancy. It seems that Barbara acted as an intermediary as it was Jean Lyon, the Countess of Angus, who later on got Barbara to arrange with Agnes a ritual using image magic to cause the death of her husband the Earl. By whatever cause, the Earl died in August 1588. Barbara also consulted Ritchie Graham to help cure her son of an illness and reportedly sent him a ring to enchant. The kind of accusations levelled against Barbara were quite typical – curing illness, influencing behaviours and outcomes, protection against malice, attempting to cause death – but because of her dealings with Agnes Sampson – which therefore implied an association with the North Berwick conspiracy – she was, like the others, charged with treason.

Barbara was tried in May 1591, and she was represented by John Moscrop and John Russell, who were employed to argue her defence. They objected to some proposed members of the jury: David Seaton, who was connected to events in Barbara's indictment. John Seaton, who was the brother of David Seaton of Tranent who had started the first accusation against Geillis Duncan. And thirdly John Douglas, who had been a hostile witness against Barbara. Barbara pled guilty to the charges of seeking help from witches but denied any involvement in treasonable plotting. She was initially found guilty of consulting but not guilty of treason. In order to delay her execution, Barbara also claimed that she was pregnant. James VI, however, was not happy with this verdict and personally addressed the jury on points of law. He also issued a warrant charging them with wilful error. The jury gathered for a second time on 9 June and this time issued a guilty verdict on the charge of treason, claiming ignorant, rather than wilful, error

Euphame MacCalzean

The charges against Euphame MacCalzean were more extensive than Barbara's: twenty-eight items including magical rituals associated with efforts to cause the death of James VI and prevent Queen Anne arriving in Scotland. Other charges were more personal and related to her unhappy marriage and her dislike of her husband, Patrick MacCalzean or Moscrop, an advocate, who changed his name from Moscrop to MacCalzean when they were married. Euphame was the illegitimate daughter (she was later legitimised) of Thomas MacCalzean, Lord Cliftonhall, also an advocate, who was a Senator in the Court of Justice. She appears to have made various efforts to rid herself of her husband, consulting several witches and carrying out a number of procedures which involved enchanting his clothes and, the ever popular, use of poison. The victim, Patrick, appears to have suffered episodes of illness and eventually left the country to seek a cure for his health – or just to get away from Euphame. On his return, she again requested help from an Irish woman, Catherine Campbell, who lived in the Canongate (now part of the Royal Mile of Edinburgh), which involved sprinkling his doublet with blood thereby enchanting it. Patrick once again fell seriously ill for some months.

As well as trying to rid herself of Patrick, Euphame used magic to help find a new, and younger, husband: Joseph Douglas, laird of Pumpherston, an estate to the east of Livingston in West Lothian. Euphame tried using love magic and sent the object of her desire several items of jewellery, which included a neck chain, belt chains, a ring and an emerald. She also tried to first injure and then, later, convince Joseph's fiancee that he was unsuitable for marriage because he was suffering from a venereal disease, using her servant Janet Drummond to carry out the task. When none of the above were successful, Euphame resorted to attempting to poison Joseph. She was also keen to get her gifts of jewellery returned as her extravagance had not paid dividends!

She was further accused of causing death by witchcraft of her nephew, her father-in-law, a young girl and several other people. Most of these other deaths were caused using enchanted cloths and clothing or image magic: Agnes Sampson was involved in using an image of Euphame's father-in-law and was consulted by Euphame on several occasions. Euphame was also accused of attending the convention at North Berwick and being involved in the attempts to sink the king's ship, by conjuring cats and throwing them into the sea.

Euphame's trial was held in June 1591, when she was defended by John Moscrop, David Ogilvie and John Russell, two of whom had defended Barbara Napier. She was found guilty on several points of her dittay notably: consulting with several witches including Agnes Sampson and Catherine Campbell, causing the death of her nephew, attempted poisoning of Joseph Douglas, using rituals to reduce the pain of childbirth, using image magic and importantly of attending the convention at North Berwick with Agnes Sampson, John Fian and others, and seeking the treasonable destruction of the king. Interestingly, she was found not guilty of trying to murder her husband. Euphame was ordered to be 'burned quick and forfeit'. This meant that Euphame was not given the benefit of being strangled before being burned – she was burned alive.

Francis Stewart, Earl of Bothwell

Francis Stewart, fifth earl of Bothwell, was the final player in the convoluted and complex North Berwick conspiracy. As early as April 1591 Bothwell had been accused of conspiring with others, notably Ritchie Graham, but it was not until Barbara Napier's verdict that Bothwell was imprisoned. It was Ritchie Graham who had given his inquisitors details about Bothwell's involvement and claimed that he had been the main instigator of the plot. Others had also named him, including Geillis Duncan and Agnes Sampson.

Bothwell was James's cousin, a nephew of James Hepburn, fourth earl of Bothwell, who had been Mary Queen of Scots', somewhat controversial, third husband. During the months before James VI left for Denmark, Bothwell had been involved in a rebellion against the king in the south, partly in support of the rebelling Catholic nobles in the north. James had a number of political and religious issues to deal with at this time, notably controlling the successors to the crown the Lennox-Stewarts and the Hamiltons, dealing with Catholic nobles such as Huntly, and establishing supremacy over the argumentative kirk. Bothwell was promoted to membership of the Council of Regency, a high status position which gave him much power and influence; indeed he was appointed admiral which gave him some responsibility and control over the Danish voyage. It is clear that James VI would later feel threatened by Bothwell's power and influence; however it was the king himself who promoted and rewarded Bothwell, whose motives were always self serving rather than altruistic.

In June 1591 Bothwell was ordered to be released but on condition that he was to be banished from the kingdom. Bothwell broke out of prison and fled to Caithness; resulting in him being declared traitor and having his property forfeited. For the next two years he evaded recapture but ultimately, in August 1593, he stood trial in Edinburgh. His indictment listed several meetings with Ritchie Graham, where Graham was requested to consult with the spirits about Bothwell's relationship with James VI. He was also accused of meeting Agnes Sampson and others associated with the North Berwick group. On 10 August 1593 Bothwell was acquitted of all the accusations contained in the dittay, and importantly of the accusation of treason and attempting to kill the king.

Perhaps it was James' own paranoia that developed the North Berwick case from a few ordinary men and women who had used magical rituals for healing or in the hope of manipulating fate, to a large number of conspirators led by an earl of the realm, whose primary target was the destruction of the king. Perhaps Bothwell was someone who was capable of developing such a dangerous plan, but to attempt something so extreme and to involve so many people would seem risky;

too many opportunities for mistakes, for leaks, and for people to turn informer.

Torture was used against several of those thought to be involved: Duncan, Sampson and Fian. There is no doubt, also, that for whatever reasons, others confessed to details and gave statements that were either directly, or interpreted as, linked to Bothwell. Ritchie Graham, interestingly, was offered immunity by Bothwell's enemies and protection if he gave evidence against Bothwell. Graham was eventually executed in February 1592, while Bothwell was on the run as an outlaw. Indeed, by this time James's actions were being criticised. Parliament met in Edinburgh and noted that public opinion was 'strongly against the king' for his complicity in the murder of the Bonnie Earl of Moray; he also had further pressures from the presbyterian wing of the kirk, led by Andrew Melville. By December of that year, Bothwell took advantage of the tension and made a public statement about his innocence, blaming the whole thing on James VI's Chancellor, Sir John Maitland of Thirlestane, and also claiming that those who had been previously executed were also innocent.

By 1593 Bothwell managed to effectively take control of James VI's government, not a easy task for someone who was declared an outlaw and liable to be taken prisoner at any point. It was a result of this political manoeuvring that Bothwell managed to bounce James into holding a trial to clear his name and restore his estates; a trial that Bothwell must have been pretty sure would deliver a verdict in his favour. The jury of two earls, seven lords and eight barons found him not guilty and declared that Ritchie Graham had been blackmailed into accusing Bothwell of witchcraft and conspiracy. Bothwell was received with 'great joy' by the people of Edinburgh, and the king was, for a time, dominated by him.

Bothwell's hour of triumph was short-lived, however, and by September 1593 he was again banished from Edinburgh under pain of treason. Bothwell's arrogance had allowed James to build support against him amongst the rest of the nobility and by 1595 Bothwell was again in trouble. Having previously been a religious vacillator, in early 1595 he was excommunicated by the Edinburgh presbytery for joining with Catholics, despite his claim that he had been forced to do so because he had lost his estates. His brother had been hanged, his estates were divided up and granted to various other nobles, and he was finally exiled, this time for good, in April 1595. He eventually died in 1612, in Italy where, it seems, he had developed a reputation for necromancy.

By this time Queen Anne had given birth to a male child – Henry. James VI had held off the threats from the northern Catholics and he had finally seen the last of the North Berwick plotters. At the same time as managing affairs of state and threats to his security, James had compiled his book on witchcraft *Daemonologie,* which was published in 1597. The following year a number of accusations surfaced in Aberdeenshire about witchcraft and witches. This time, however, the king was not the target.

Andrew Mann
1598

Andrew Mann (also recorded as Andro Man in written records), from Tarbruith in Aberdeenshire, was found guilty of witchcraft in 1598, a year after James VI published his book on witchcraft *Daemonologie*. Mann was one of several people from this area of the country accused, tried and convicted of witchcraft in 1598. *Daemonologie* was published in Edinburgh the previous year but was probably

Daemonologie, *1597.*

compiled and written during the peak of the North Berwick trials, as many of the details and descriptions appear to be directly related to a number of the North Berwick accused.

It is clear that after 1603 James may have been more sceptical about witchcraft and witch trials; however in the early 1590s he was fully convinced of the reality of witches and their powers. He firmly argued that Holy Scripture supported his claims about witchcraft, that it should be punished severely, and that it was the responsibility of magistrates – and particularly Godly magistrates such as himself – to ensure these punishments were carried out. James also included Revelationary references to the end of days and how this would be manifested; this was certainly in keeping with other day of judgement theories expressed during the 1590s.

While the Aberdeenshire episode has some chronological correspondence with the timing of the publication of James's book, it is unlikely that the book itself sparked the accusations, as they first started in February/March 1597. Andrew's accusation was first made in October of that year. *Daemonologie* was not published until autumn of 1597. Nevertheless there are descriptions in Andrew's confession which are very similar to James's references to the Book of Revelation, the final book of *The Bible* which predicts Armageddon, a final battle between the forces of evil and good, the Devil and Christ. There are also some similarities with Alison Pearson's relationship with the fairies or elves, as both parties claimed to have received their knowledge and skill of healing from the fairies or the 'good neighbours' as they were known.

Mann would appear to have been around seventy years old when he was accused, as he confessed to having been a consort to the Queen of Elfame for over sixty years. According to Mann's testimony, the queen of elves or fairies, appeared to him when he was a boy, and requested some assistance as she was about to give birth to a baby. In return he was given the gift of prophecy and healing.

Mann claimed that he had the power to cure almost all ailments in man and beast except 'stand deid', and his confession contained many descriptions of healing rituals. This was not the only reward as Mann also described how as an adult, he had a sexual relationship with the queen and fathered several children with her. However, it would appear that he was only one of several different consorts as he also described how she would pick any male of the court – young or old – to be king for the day, implying that she was quite generous with her sexual favours.

The descriptions of healing rituals are most interesting and demonstrate a sound understanding of the concept of transference. Illness or bad luck was often claimed to have been caused by enchantment or bewitchment, either deliberate or accidental. The antidote, or cure, was transference of the bad luck or illness on to some other object or person. Mann advised Alexander Simpson to pass forward through a piece of unwoven or untreated yarn or wool. After this, a cat was passed backwards through the same yarn, nine times. As this was done Mann recited oral blessings – orisons or orations – over the man and animal. When the man recovered his health, the cat took ill and died. Somewhat harsh on the cat, of course, but cats were more expendable than other animals.

Mann's description of the fairy court and Queen of Elfame has some similar features to that of Alison Pearson and others. However, his confession gave a far more detailed account of fairy society and their appearance: '[they] have shapes and clothes like men' but they were also much stronger than mortals. Like Alison's fairies, these good neighbours enjoyed fine food and singing and dancing, and they also rode on white ponies. Mann described meeting not only fairies at these assemblies but also ghosts. The cultural and literary link between fairies and ghosts is strong: Alison Pearson's cousin/uncle William Simpson may have been a ghost. One explanation for fairies is that they were, in fact, the ghosts of dead people; those who had, for some reason, been unable to progress beyond this physical realm.

A number of confessions from accused witches referred to both ghosts and fairies within the same narrative, which suggests that, culturally, the lines between the two spirit beings were blurred. Whilst there are other explanations for the existence of fairies within Scottish folk narrative – particularly those related to nature spirits – the fairy/ghost one seems the strongest. Mann's ghosts were an interesting bunch and included James IV, the king who died at

Flodden in 1513, and True Thomas or Thomas the Rhymer, who had something of a reputation for prophecy and implying that his skill was linked to an association with fairies, although Andrew may have been familiar with the legends surrounding Thomas the Rhymer and that the legendary seer had reputedly spend seven years in the fairy realm.

The more unusual items of Mann's testimony related to his descriptions of a devil figure and his references to the Day of Judgement; both highly religious and quite unorthodox. The devil/spirit was called Christonday, according to Mann's account, although he was not the only accused from Aberdeen who used the term. Not only could Christonday take the form of a man but it also appeared as a stag. Christonday, who could be summoned by Mann when he spoke the word 'Benedicte', was: an angel in white, the Devil, a 'hynd knight', a consort of the Queen of Elfame, and God's son-in-law.

This spirit also told Mann about the future and that the following year (presumably 1598) would be a hard year, but that it would be followed by fourteen good ones. In his dittay, it records that Mann claimed on the final day the 'fire will burn the water and the earth and make all plain' and that 'every man will have his own dittay, written in his own book, to accuse himself'. Christonday was clearly interpreted by the authorities and jury as the Devil: Christonday had left a mark on the third finger of Mann's right hand and Mann reportedly would leave part of his rig unploughed and left as offering to the hynd knight. Another version of this practice was known as the 'Guid Man's Croft': some land was left as an offering to the Devil as a means of protection for the rest of the crop.

Mann was tried in January 1598 and was found guilty although not on all charges: it was not recorded which charges were proven and which were not. Presumably, as with others from Aberdeen episode, he was executed in the usual manner.

The Erskines
1613-14

The following case involves a dispute over property, namely the wealthy barony and estate of Dun, which is located three miles north-west of Montrose in Angus in the east of Scotland. Although the case did include witchcraft, this crime can be seen simply as a straight case of murder by poisoning.

The lands of Dun were long held by the Erskines, the property having come to them in 1375, and they had a castle, although this was demolished when the fine House of Dun, a classical mansion, was built in 1730 by the architect William Adam. A prominent member of the Erskines was John, a scholar and reformer in the time of Mary, Queen of Scots, but branches of the family came into conflict

House of Dun, the mansion replaced the Erskine's original castle.

early in the seventeenth century, a conflict which led to witchcraft, poisoning, murder and execution.

When John Erskine, the ninth laird of Dun, died in 1610 without a son, his nephew, also called John, stood to inherit the property and title. John and his brother Alexander were boys at the time and were put into the care and tutelage of a relative, another John Erskine, this John being the minister of Ceres. Robert, their uncle and the brother of the ninth laird, had hoped to gain that position for himself, as he would have benefited financially and he would also have had the heir to the estate in his power. In truth, he was angry and vengeful that he had been passed over for a more distant relation.

Robert plotted with his three sisters (the boy's aunts) – Isobel, Annas and Helen – to remove the obstacle to him inheriting Dun; presumably the sisters would have benefited from Robert's generosity. Firstly they went to a man, David Blewhouse, offering him the princely sum of five hundred silver merks and some land to help in their scheme, but he refused. Then two of the sisters went to a local woman, Janet Irving, who resided at Muiralehouse and who had a reputation for being a witch. Janet promised that she could give them herbs which she assured the conspirators would solve their problem.

The herbs were soaked in ale and the poisoned drink was then given to the two lads at a house in Montrose. Both the boys immediately fell violently ill and started terrible vomiting. The heir John Erskine suffered an appalling illness: his skin went black, his inner parts were consumed and he wasted away in agony until his death. It is said that before he finally he expired, he said, perhaps rather articulately for someone in their death throes: 'Woe is me, that ever I had right of succession to my lands or living! For had I been born some poor cottar's son, I had not been so treated, nor wicked practices had plotted against me for my lands!' Alexander, the younger lad, was also very sick and poorly but somehow he survived.

Foul play was, of course suspected, and in 1613 Robert Erskine was interrogated by the Privy Council and confessed to his part in the lads' poisoning, implicating his three sisters, as well as Janet Irving and the others involved. After a trial he was found guilty and was executed by beheading at the Mercat Cross in Edinburgh. The following year his sisters were also tried and were also found guilty. Isobel and Annas were beheaded in Edinburgh, but Helen's part seems to have been less significant and, also because she showed much remorse, her sentence was commuted to banishment, on pain of death if she ever returned to mainland Scotland (she went to Orkney). Janet Irving was tried, and was probably executed although her case appears to have been handled locally so there are no detailed records.

In truth, although the Erskines were accused of consulting with a witch, this was a case of murder by poisoning for profit and that was enough in itself to get them executed, which is why they were not killed in the normal way for a witch by throttling and burning. It is not clear which poison Janet Irving gave to Robert Erskine and his sisters to use on their nephews, but it was certainly powerful, if not entirely effective.

Alexander Erskine went on to become the eleventh laird of Dun, and was knighted and was made a Privy Councillor, although in his later years he was plagued by debt and he died in reduced circumstances in London.

Margaret Wallace
1622

The case of Margaret Wallace from Glasgow is less about wicked, demonic witches and more about community rivalry and tensions. Statistically, those accused of witchcraft were often old, poor, unmarried and female. This may have been the broad pattern but as the accounts in this book have highlighted this was not always the case: 'witches' could also be young or middle-aged; they could have high status and potential wealth; they might be married; they could be male.

Although many of the accused came from rural or agricultural/fishing communities, those suspected of being witches could also come from towns where trading and the marketplace were of paramount importance to the community. Status was important in seventeenth-century Scotland and society was very hierarchical: the feudal system which had developed from the eleventh century meant that levels of society had distinct rights and obligations, and some also had certain privileges. One such group, or level, was that of burgess: burgesses were freemen of burghs, and as such were allowed economic and political advantages over the rest of the burgh population. Merchant burgesses regarded themselves as the most privileged; certainly higher status than craftsmen.

Margaret Wallace was the wife of a merchant

burgess – John Dunning (or Dyning) – in Glasgow and was tried for witchcraft in 1622; her indictment also included the standard accusations of sorcery, charming, incantation, soothsaying and abusing of her fellow citizens. Some of her trouble seems to have been caused by the fact that her husband borrowed an ellwand – a measuring stick – which he broke, which caused arguments and complaints. Another part of her case revolved around consultation with another woman who was a 'known witch', about the taking-off and laying-on of illnesses. However, Margaret also seems to have been quite a disputatious individual and quarrelled with several people in the neighbourhood, which did not help her case and seemed to contribute to her reputation. Another aspect seems to have been that there were disagreements about accounts or unpaid money due to Margaret and John, so as a couple their popularity and reputation may have been somewhat questionable before 1622.

Some of the details of the accusations illustrate the petty squabbling and backbiting which must have been quite commonplace in burgh communities. Unfortunately the case escalated and, despite being able to afford defence counsel and with the prosecution case including accusations of murder, events turned very serious indeed for Margaret. She was arrested without warrant by John Dickson, and ultimately executed by being strangled and burnt at Castle Hill in Edinburgh.

Many of the accusers in 1622 were other Glasgow craft and merchant burgesses, with whom

Margaret, or her husband John, had had a falling out. With burgh communities being tightly-knit and often comprising extended families and relatives, the arguments and disputes involved more than just the original protagonists. Margaret also seems to have been in trouble with the church and was called in front of the kirk session for 'rayling' (presumably confronting and complaining about people angrily and argumentatively) around 1613 or 1614, and it seems that many of the complaints went back some years before 1622. The indictment noted that Margaret had been 'eight or nine years' a common consulter with witches.

One of the main pursuers was Alexander Boig, a smith, who had fallen out with Margaret and her husband over non-payment for an anvil. It seems that Boig may have owed the couple money and when he did not pay up, it was claimed that Margaret cursed Boig in the hearing of Boig's master, Sir George Elphinstone. Later one of Boig's children took ill and died. Another charge also related to Margaret's cursing of Cuthbert Greig, a cooper and fellow burgess, who subsequently suffered an acute and debilitating illness. After some time Margaret visited Greig, at his request, and was asked to help him. According to Greig she felt his wrist, laid her hand on his chest, and muttered some words. On the next visit she took him by the arm and told him he was cured and able to walk.

The charge of laying-on and taking-off illnesses featured more than once, and unfortunately for Margaret the taking-off did not always work, which meant that families accused her of causing the death of their relatives. One example was that of Robert Muir. It was alleged that Margaret had cursed Muir, saying: 'You shall go home to thy house and shall bleed at thy nose a quart of blood, but shall not die until you send for me and ask my forgiveness'. Muir died shortly afterwards of a sudden illness.

A third, important strand of Margaret's actions involved her association and consultation of a recently convicted witch, Christian Graham, who had been executed the previous year. One of the charges claimed that Margaret was 'airt and pairt' with Christian and received from Christian coloured silk and worsted to use in witchcraft rituals against those whom Margaret bore a grudge or envied. In another detailed accusation it was claimed that Margaret took ill at Alexander Vallange's house and Margaret sent for Christian who cured her using 'devilish charms'. Presumably Margaret felt that her illness had been caused by the Vallange household because Margaret returned to their house, accompanied by Christian, where she met Margaret Vallange, the young daughter – perhaps the meeting was just coincidence? Soon after the girl took a fit of illness or faint and Margaret advised the girl's mother to consult Christian, which the mother refused to do. Christian seems to have visited the house anyway and made crosses and signs over the girl, who then recovered.

Margaret was relatively unusual in that she could afford to engage lawyers to defend her. Her defence advocates – Thomas Nicolson, Alexander

Peebles and Robert Lermonth – attempted to argue against or object to each of the charges on the dittay. They also objected to some of the members of the jury, one of whom was John Dickson, who made the initial arrest and who had a long-standing animosity with Margaret's husband. Another juryman was William Anderson, who the defence argued had a dispute with Margaret over non-payment for some drugs which she had sold him. Interestingly, it is recorded that Margaret had some skill in surgery, which was quite unusual for this time, although just what this skill was was not explained. Both Dickson and Anderson having sworn that they had been purged of any 'partial counsall' were allowed on the jury. The defence argument that Walter Stirling, who was the brother-in-law of the deceased Robert Muir, was unlikely to be impartial was accepted and he was replaced.

The defence argued that many of the points on the dittay were not relevant, that events were coincidental, and that they did not prove that Margaret was a witch or practised witchcraft. Arguments based on demonological authorities such as Delrio were used by both prosecution and defence regarding what constituted witchcraft. The defence argued that the prosecution could not specify how the 'witchcraft' had been carried out as they made no reference to the use of signs, crosses, pictures, powders, and Satanic invocations in the dittay, therefore there was no proof. They complained that the reference to laying-on and to taking-off was too general and did not explain the means whereby it was done. The prosecution reply to both objections was that there was no need to specify how something was done as witches knew how they carried out their own craft, so the charges were sufficiently precise and relevant

The reliability of Margaret's 'pretended' confession was argued over. The prosecution claimed that she had confessed to Cuthbert Greig in his house. The defence argued that this was not possible to prove and, indeed, she denied being in his house, and therefore the confession was inadmissible. There was nothing in her alleged confession about having made a demonic pact or having Devil's marks, both of which were regarded as standard proof of demonic witchcraft by this time. They complained that the allegation made by Christian Graham about Margaret being a witch was unreliable, as her confession was not made before judge with authority or commission to do so. They also pointed out that while Margaret may have had knowledge that Christian was a witch, that did not necessarily imply that Margaret was a witch or knew witchcraft. Margaret's consultation of Christian for advice about her own illness suggested that she thought that she had been bewitched herself.

Her lawyers also objected to some of the evidence which appeared to be based on hearsay and second-hand accounts: 'he said and she said'. They complained about the competency of witnesses and lack of corroboration, noting that some of their statements had not been recorded in front of a competent judge or official representative. Some of the witnesses were also young, but the prosecution was able to refer to legal precedents which allowed particular or unusual procedural matters in cases of witchcraft.

Witness testimonies and evidence was also quite vague and often seemed circumstantial. One example was Andrew Muir who spoke about the curing of a child, Margaret Muir, by Christian Graham. He said he saw Christian Graham come out of the house, he then went inside and ate chicken with others there. Margaret Wallace then came in and a roast goose was put on the table. He decided to leave at that point and knew nothing further.

For the unfortunate Margaret her bad temper and verbal haranguing did her no favours. Several witnesses described her cursing those who had angered her, and any subsequent bad luck or ill health was attributed to Margaret: in her case, words were more powerful than actions. Some of her curses may have had some justification – after Greig had slandered Christian and Margaret as witches, she replied to him: 'false landlubber loun that thou art, says thou that Christian Graham and I shall be burnt for witches? I vow to God I shall do thee an evil turn'. It would seem Margaret was invoking the help of God rather than the Devil, given the serious implications of such a slander. The witness to this exchange of words, George Pollok, said that he knew nothing about what happened before or after and did not see Margaret go into Greig's house.

Margaret was found guilty of causing Greig's illness; of consulting Christian Graham to cure herself and casting the illness on to Alexander Vallange's child, later curing the child; of curing Margaret Muir's illness, again consulting Christian; and of casting a 'cruel sickness' on Alexander Boig's child. She was also found guilty on the general point of consulting with witches: Christian Graham, Katherine Blair and others. Finally she was guilty of using witchcraft to cure herself and friends, and for inflicting diseases on several people for whom she bore any hatred. She was ordered to be taken to the Castle Hill of Edinburgh (now the Castle Esplanade, where the tattoo is held) and there strangled to death and then burnt in March of 1622.

Edinburgh Castle. Many found guilty of witchcraft were executed on what is now the Esplanade of the castle.

This case is less about being wicked and evil and more about being verbally aggressive and argumentative. Margaret's reputation did not help her defence but were any of her actions demonic? Her arguing seems to have been no worse than some of her neighbours; they seemed to give as good as they got. Certainly her curses threatened injury and misfortune, but she never confessed that she had renounced her baptism or had a relationship with the Devil. Indeed Margaret continually denied being a witch. Despite affording a defence counsel and denying all the charges, the testimony of her neighbours and community convinced the jury. Demonic witchcraft was undoubtedly a threat for seventeenth-century society, but equally it could be used as an excuse to rid a community of an unpopular and frightening woman.

Maggie Wall and Kate MacNiven

Two intriguing cases come from Perthshire, intriguing because, although they are both well and widely known, there is no corroborating or contemporary written evidence to support either.

The first is Maggie Wall. There is a monument to her on the B8062 road between Auchterarder and Dunning, about 0.5 miles from the latter village. The monument consists of a stepped plinth surmounted by a pillar and is topped by a small cross. Written in white is: 'Maggie Wall burnt here 1657 as a witch'.

So, who was Maggie Wall? Although Dunning

Maggie Wall monument, near Dunning.

53

was not immune from witchcraft accusations, there are no records of a Margaret or Maggie Wall, Walls or Wallace, so the name, at least, may be apocryphal and the monument may be a memorial used to represent those who were executed than any one particular person. The writing is regularly repainted and flowers and other items are left at the monument. Maggie is said to be the last victim of the witchcraft accusations to be burnt alive, although – as noted elsewhere – it was usual to throttle the victim first.

It is possible to visit the monument, although parking on the road is limited. Coins and other items, including candles, are left at the monument.

KATE MACNIVEN

Another well-known story is that of Kate MacNiven, also known as the Witch of Monzie.

So, who was Kate?

Kate was reputedly a nurse at Monzie Castle, which lies a couple of miles north and east of Crieff, also in Perthshire, and she attained a reputation as a witch, who – among other things – could turn herself into a bee. Kate was seized, taken up a hill known as the Knock of Crieff to the north of the town, and was then rolled down the steep slope in a barrel. The slope down which was pushed is now called Kate McNiven's Craig. She was then burnt at a place near an ancient five-foot standing stone (now known as Kate MacNiven's Stone), which is located to the south of the drive to that goes to Monzie Castle.

One of the Grahams of Inchbrackie (which is a neighbouring property) tried to save Kate, but to

Monzie Castle, Kate was reputedly nurse to the family.

no avail. In thanks, she spat out a bead into Graham's hand. The bead turned out to be a sapphire, which was used as the stone in a ring, and she told Graham that as long as his family kept the bead they would prosper (in truth, they may have but Inchbrackie Castle has gone and the lands were sold in 1882). She also cursed the laird of Monzie and his family, another branch of the Grahams, did lose the property. Monzie Castle survives and is still a family home, although not of the Grahams.

Again it is not clear whether Kate MacNiven was a real person or a conflation of witchcraft stories. There are no contemporary written records for her, and the date of her unpleasant death is given variously as 1563, 1615 or 1715. MacNiven or NicNiven was also the name given to the Queen of the Fairies or of Elfame.

Whatever the truth of it, Kate MacNiven's name now appears on the Ordnance Survey map of the area.

Isobel Gowdie
1662

Isobel Gowdie is one of the best-known cases from
the witchcraft trials in Scotland, partly because her
long and detailed confession is especially interesting
and suggestive, but also because her case was used
by later authors to construct an ancient and enduring
pagan or demonic belief system, not least by
Margaret Murray, although her idea of a fertility cult
has been soundly criticised by many in recent years.
It was claimed that Isobel's testimony confirmed
what many now believe as Satanic practice – an
inversion of Christian belief – such as a coven of
thirteen witches, a renunciation of Christ with a
Satanic baptism, copulation with the Devil, flying,

The Devil seducing a woman (1489).

shape shifting, controlling the weather, and murder by magical means, including using an effigy of the victim.

Isobel's story has also inspired her inclusion as a character in several novels and songs, as well as an orchestral work by James MacMillan, called 'The Confession of Isobel Gowdie', premiered in 1990.

Isobel Gowdie originally resided in Auldearn, which lies a few miles east of Nairn in the north of Scotland. Some have described her as a beautiful, red-haired young housewife at the time of her prosecution, although in 1662 Isobel was certainly no longer young, especially for seventeenth-century Scotland. Although it is not known when she was born, a commission for investigating Isobel was issued in July 1643, some nineteen years before her confessions in April and May of 1662. In her statements, she said that she only became involved in malefice after she was married, so it is likely by the time of her trial she was in her fifties. The source for her being beautiful or red haired is not clear. Her name is recorded as Issobell in the documents of the time, and her surname can also be spelt 'Goudie'.

Isobel was the daughter of a lawyer, and she was married to John Gilbert, a kirk elder and a tenant-farmer on the lands of Lochloy, about a mile or so to the north of Auldearn. Married women in Scotland retained their maiden names, which is why she is known as Isobel Gowdie and not Isobel Gilbert. The lands were rented from the local landowner, John Hay of Park and Lochloy. Isobel was of the middle order in Scottish society, and would have been relatively wealthy compared to many. That she was unhappy in her marriage, and generally with her life, seems apparent from her subsequent behaviour, whatever the truth of her statements. When she met another local woman reputedly involved in witchcraft, Margaret Brodie, believed to be the daughter of the laird of Brodie and a gypsy woman, Isobel strayed – all according to her own testimony – into a life of devilry, deceit and wantonness.

On the road to Drumduan, a place half a mile to the south-west of Lochloy, Isobel encountered the Devil, according to her own testimony. To impress her and to seduce her into renouncing her Christian faith, the Devil predicted that the following day the fertile lands of Culbin, on the shores of the Moray Firth, would be inundated with sand during a storm, which they duly were, ruining the harvest. Indeed, as the century proceeded, the encroachment of sand increasingly became a problem until virtually the whole estate was covered in dunes; today the highest sand dunes in Scotland are at Culbin. Isobel perhaps took this event as a sign of the Devil's veracity and power.

Isobel then went to Auldearn Kirk, where she met the Devil again, as well as Margaret Brodie and more of his followers. She found the Devil standing at the reader's desk in the kirk, with a black book in his hand, and he then baptised her, using her own blood. This blood he had sucked out of a 'Devil's' mark on Isobel's shoulder, spitting it into her hand and then sprinkling it over her head and making a symbol, baptising her under her new name, 'Janet'. She described the Devil as being a 'meikle, black, roch man' (large, black, rough man) with cloven feet.

Isobel consummated her relationship with the Devil a little while later near Inshoch Castle (a mile

Inshoch Castle: Isobel reputedly met the Devil near here.

or so to the south-east of Lochloy), and also described many other amorous encounters, including with the Devil in the form of a deer. She described the Devil as having a member which was great and long, and that many of the younger women enjoyed sex with the Devil more than with their husbands. She explained that, while out on her diabolic and wanton escapades, she managed to deceive her husband into thinking she was still in bed with him, or had even accompanied him to church, by various means, including a shadow-self, a body-double, and turning herself into a jackdaw and slipping away. Consequently her husband John Gilbert remained ignorant of her behaviour, which was fortunate for him as he might also have become involved in the accusation and shared her fate.

Isobel said that each witch had a spirit to look after them and carry out their will; her spirit was called the Red Reiver and was dressed in black. She reported that there were thirteen in their group or coven, that there was a male and a female leader, and that she became the head of the coven at the Devil's command. As well as at Auldearn, they also met at Hill of Earlseat and in the kirk of Nairn, and there were Grand Meetings at the end of each quarter year. She also told that the Devil beat them at their meetings, and that large sums of money given to them by Satan changed into horse dung within a day.

Isobel claimed that she and others could fly, and used this to get into people's houses to steal food and drink. To fly, they needed to recite, 'Horse and hattock, in the Devil's name,' with the straw between their feet. This has been interpreted by some as perhaps being a reference to a broomstick. They could also change shape, taking the form of animals, such as a jackdaw (kea in her words), a cat or a hare. The incantation used to transform into a hare was:

> I shall go into a hare,
> With sorrow and such and meikle care;
> And I shall go in the Devil's name,
> Ay while I come home again.

(meikle = great)

To restore their usual form, the following would be said:

> Hare, hare, God send thee care.
> I am in a hare's likeness now,
> But I shall be in a woman's likeness even now.

They also stole milk from beasts, by passing a tether between the cow's or sheep's legs, as well as thieving ale by magical means, taking it for themselves; the spell could be reversed by removing the tether. Similarly they stole crops; however one of the spells employed was much less pleasant.

At the kirk of Nairn, Isobel reported, with others, taking the body of an unbaptised baby and chopping it up into small pieces and combining it with their own nail clippings, grain and kale. This

Witches casting a spell using the corpse of a child.

they used to take the corn from a farmer, leaving only empty husks, and sharing the crop among themselves. At another meeting, she and her coven took paddocks (toads), and yoked them together to plough a field, leaving the ground only capable of growing thistles and briars. At a dye-house, they performed a ritual using a thread with three knots, to remove dye, turning what remained black. Nor was their thieving confined to land: they also purloined fishermen's catches, taking the larger fish for their own, by repeating three times:

> The fishers are gone to the sea,
> And they will bring home fish to me;
> They will bring them home in the boat,
> But they shall get of them but the smaller sort.

They could also reputedly control the weather, and raised a wind using a spell using a cloth and a beetle in water.

Isobel also told of their use fairy darts or elf shot (what is now known to be prehistoric stone or flint arrow heads that were found in the area – and in many other parts of the country). According to her, these could be used to kill a person when the victim was struck with elf shot, although the arrow head had to be flicked in a special way using the thumb. Isobel said that she had slain several men this way, although just for her own pleasure, giving the commission the names of her victims. In her statement, she claimed that the Devil gave elves instructions on how to use and make elf shot, and

The Archer-Witch, using enchanted arrows.

that the soul of a victim went to heaven but the body remained on earth. Indeed, the elf shot was manufactured by small hump-backed elf boys. She also said they recited the following verse when using the elf shot:

> I shoot yon man in the Devil's name,
> He shall no win heal hame!
> And this shall always be true,
> There shall not be a bit of him alive.

As well as the Devil, Isobel met the elves, going down into a huge chamber in the Downie Hills, where at a great gathering she met the Queen of the Fairies or Elfame, describing her as being dressed in brown and white, and the King, 'a braw, well favoured man with a broad face'. There were great bulls with the elves, a sign of their evident fantastic wealth and prosperity.

More seriously, Isobel apparently had a dispute with John Hay of Lochloy and Park, the local laird and her landlord. Some have suggested that he made improper advances towards her and that he would not repair dilapidated buildings on her rented farm. Along with others, Isobel made a clay figure of Hay's son, roasting it and baking it in a fire. She claimed she spoke the following verse:

> In the Devil's name,
> We pour this water among this meal,
> For long dwyning and ill health,
> We put it into the fire,
> That it may be burnt both stick and stour,
> It shall be burnt with our will,
> As any stickle upon a kill.
>
> (dwyning = dwindling   stour = ashes, dirt
> stickle = stubble   kill = kiln)

This was to slay Hay's male children, who reportedly then died. When Hay's wife had further boys these thrived for only six months or so before they too withered and died.

Henry Forbes, the local minister, was also reputedly put under a spell and was afflicted with a wasting disease, although he later recovered and was one of those in attendance when Isobel made her confessions.

Isobel made four statements in April and May of 1662 about her unsavoury behaviour, apparently without torture or force being used, although the truth of that can never been known. Why she would have chosen to do such a thing under her own volition is not clear. This was at the height of the witchcraft accusations and prosecutions, and conviction would lead to her death and that of anyone implicated with her.

In the commission granted in 1643 it did state that Isobel should be healthy in mind and body and that no duress was to be used. She was taken into custody on 12 April 1662, and the statements were made from the next day before a commission of local lairds, ministers and men of the parish and were recorded by John Innes, a public notary. As the commission was granted nearly nineteen years before, however, it must have been well known in the area about the accusations and about the suspicions surrounding Isobel Gowdie and her friends and contemporaries.

Her statements implicated the other twelve people in her coven, and eventually more than forty women and men were included in accusations (although these were mostly from the confession of another local woman, Janet Braidhead, who confessed at the same time as Isobel).

Isobel's final fate, however, is not recorded, nor is that of her co-accused. If she had survived unscathed until after the trial, however, it is very likely that she was throttled and then her mortal remains were burnt, along with the other accused, and their ashes were scattered on unconsecrated ground.

Mary Lamont
1662

Another case of 1662 involved the teenager, Mary Lamont (or Lawmont in documents). Mary was accused of witchcraft, along with Margaret Duff and others, from the parish of Inverkip in the west of Scotland. Part of her case involved an interesting collision between different belief systems: Christian, diabolic and what might be called traditional, the latter perhaps harking back to a pagan or at least a pre-Christian origin.

Much of Mary's apparent confession of 1662 consisted of elements found in other accusations, although she was quite young when her reputed wickedness first asserted itself and that would make the case memorable in itself. Mary was from the Greenock or Gourock area, and she was about thirteen when she claimed she embarked on her career of malefice. Accusations included renunciation of her Christian faith and being baptised by Satan with the name 'Clowts', stealing milk by magical means, and shape shifting into a cat. She also apparently confessed to having sex with the Devil several times when he appeared to her in the form of a large brown dog, marks being left on her when the demonic animal nipped her side.

She also confessed to, along with a group of other witches, trying to throw the Kempock Stone into the sea to sink ships in the Firth of Clyde and bring catastrophe to the fishing fleet. The Kempock Stone, now widely known as Granny Kempock Stone although formerly as Lang Stane, stands on Kempock Point at Gourock on the southern shore of the Firth of Clyde, and is a six-foot high standing stone. It can be reached up a winding flight of narrow steps from Gourock's main shopping street. The stone bears a (little) resemblance to an old hunched woman wearing a hood, hence its name Granny. Good luck rituals were associated with the stone, and it was used by both fishermen and by newly wed couples.

The ritual involved fetching a bucket of sand from the beach, then walking around the stone seven times withershins (anti-sunwise) with the bucket while chanting and singing. Fishermen performed the ritual to ensure good weather, a favourable wind, and a large catch of fish, while betrothed couples or newly weds hoped for a fruitful marriage with lots of healthy children.

In truth, this ritual would have been frowned upon by the church of seventeenth-century Scotland, and in many parishes this kind of practice, such as visiting shrines and wells, was deliberately discouraged and even prevented, being thought of (at best) as superstitious. It is not clear what the nature of the chanted verse was, but if this was interpreted as an incantation, this ritual could have been seen as witchcraft and those taking part prosecuted for malefice. That Mary and her companions, and by implication the Devil, might try to get rid of the Granny Kempock Stone is interesting

Witches casting a spell to cause hail (1489).

in that it suggests the power of the stone was not in the domain of either Satan or of Christ.

Although the official records are missing or lost, Mary Lamont, Margaret Duff and others of the accused were most likely found guilty of witchcraft and were executed. Some say that an apparition of Mary, accompanied by the Devil, can still be seen some nights during the full moon, dancing around Granny Kempock Stone.

Demonic Possession Cases from 1696

CHRISTIAN SHAW, BARGARRAN 1696-97
MARGARET MURDOCH, AND MARGARET LAIRD,
PAISLEY 1699-1700
PATRICK MORTON, PITTENWEEM 1704-05

There are a number of interesting and unusual features in the accusations and prosecutions of Janet Corphat (or Cornfoot) and Beatrix Laing, from Pittenweem in Fife. One, because the date of their trial was relatively late, 1705, which was well after the peak in prosecution of alleged witches seen in

Pittenweem, scene of an infamous witchcraft episode in 1704-05.

1662. After this trials and prosecutions began to decline. This did not, however, mean that concerns and fears about witches and witchcraft had disappeared. On the contrary, although trials may have reduced, accusations continued, even well after the rewording of the Witchcraft Act in 1736-37.

Secondly, it is also interesting because it involved a relatively young teenage 'victim', Patrick Morton, who claimed that he had been bewitched and possessed.

There were four teenagers, or pre-teenagers, in Scotland who claimed they were possessed, the most notorious being the 1696-97 case of Christian Shaw of Bargarran, in Renfrewshire, who accused a large number of people of bewitching her and causing her to manifest strange fits where her body would go rigid and suffer convulsions, she would vomit hair, straw, coal and other objects, and she would start speaking to invisible spirits.

Two years later there was another case in the Paisley area where two girls – Margaret Murdoch and Margaret Laird – displayed very similar symptoms: rigidity, spasms, vomiting, loss of speech. More than twenty people were accused of witchcraft. The links between the Renfrewshire and Paisley cases are not coincidental as there had been much publicity about Christian Shaw and printed pamphlets describing events had been in circulation. Also one of the commissioners – Sir John Maxwell of Pollok – was involved in both the 1696-97 and 1698-99 investigations and trials.

Patrick Morton is therefore part of a trend, albeit a short-lived one, that saw a number of people executed on the words of teenage witnesses.

CHRISTIAN SHAW

In August 1696 when Christian Shaw was about ten she began to experience strange fits which lasted for about a year. She was seen to experience spasms when her body would jerk and her back arch. Her explanation for her symptoms was that she had been cursed by a family servant, Katherine Campbell. Katherine was from the Highlands so spoke Gaelic, not a language that Christian would understand. Christian had reprimanded Katherine over some incident involving milk, which Christian accused Katherine of stealing or spoiling in some way. According to Christian, Katherine had cursed her by saying: 'The Devil harle your soul through Hell'.

As Christian's symptoms worsened she was examined by apothecaries and physicians – she was even taken to Glasgow to be examined by a leading physician, Sir Matthew Brisbane. Undoubtedly, the reports that she vomited nails, animal hair, bones, straw and coal paint a distressing picture of the suffering of a young, pubertal, girl. Her body spasms must have caused her family great anxiety, and when she accused Katherine of cursing her that must have seemed an acceptable explanation. As a subject of speculation and interest, people heard about Christian's condition and many inquisitive visitors came to the house to see her. Ministers prayed over her and during these episode reportedly she would

Pandaemonium (1684), illustrating ideas about witches.

become extremely violent, claiming that she could see and engage in theological debates with the Devil. She then began to recite biblical verses, particularly from the Book of Job. Her ability to refer to and quote from Job, which described similar suffering and torment, seems a tad advanced for a young girl, even one brought up in a Christian household in seventeenth-century Scotland, and perhaps more than a little convenient for those around her who might have been using the case for their own purposes.

Christian named up to twenty-four people who were involved in the bewitchment, and the Privy Council issued a commission in January 1697. People were questioned, including some children, and confessed to sabbats and meetings which were held at Bargarran Orchard. They claimed that they had caused the capsizing of the Erskine ferry boat and the death of John Hardie, a minister at Dumbarton.

In the end, only seven of the accused were tried: Katherine Campbell, Agnes Nasmith, Margaret Fulton, Margaret Lang, John and James Lindsay – whose aliases were, it was claimed, the bishop and the curate – and another John Lindsay. One man John Reid hanged himself before his trial. Agnes Nasmith was said to have a reputation as an ignorant and malicious old widow who was given to cursing her neighbours. All of them, apart from Reid, were executed at Paisley in May 1697.

Christian made a full 'recovery' from her experience and after being widowed she returned to the family home and was one of the founders of the Bargarran Thread Company, which helped lead to the establishment of Paisley as a world-famous cotton and textile production area. Christian's contribution to wealth of the town was very important. However, she is better known for her role in the accusation and trial of witches particularly as subsequent publications about her sufferings added to the controversy. 'A True narrative of the Sufferings and Relief of a Young Girle; Strangely molested by Evil Spirits and their instruments in the West: With a preface and postscript containing Reflections on what is most Material or Curious either in the history or trial of the Seven Witches who were condemn'd to be Execute in the country' was published anonymously in Edinburgh, the following year. To an extent it is this account which gave the case increased attention – even perhaps leading to 'copy-cat' cases – especially given the general overall decline in prosecutions during the latter decades of the seventeenth century and the early years of the eighteenth century.

And indeed the controversy did not end with the end of the witch trials. The 'Narrative' has given later historians, and even contemporary writers, reason to accuse Christian of being an impostor, that her claims of possession and torment were mere pretence; a deliberate and malicious act. That a girl of ten or eleven was able to trick learned and educated ministers, theologians, physicians, and lawyers into believing that she was bewitched does seem somewhat unbelievable, nevertheless more educated men of the time were convinced of the reality of demonic magic than were sceptical about it, and so these men were at least prepared to accept the explanation of possession.

Another explanation that has been posed is that Christian may have been suffering from a mental illness, possibly hysteria, or experiencing some hormonal changes due to puberty, resulting in emotional turmoil. She could also have been suffering from some form of epilepsy; however this explanation seems less likely in the face of her recovery and longevity with, apparently, no further epileptic seizures. One problem is how did she manage to perform the vomiting or spasms, the flying around the room, and the speaking in tongues, if they were all tricks? Did she have an accomplice or accomplices or was she perhaps a victim as well? Was any of Christian's behaviour genuine or was it all exaggerated? Could she have been manipulated by others, particularly the ministers who were witnesses to her torment and who were the likely authors of the anonymous pamphlet?

It has been suggested that these could have been Andrew Turner, minister at Erskine, and James Brisbane, minister at Kilmacolm, who was related to the physician Matthew Brisbane. Another possible author was Francis Grant, Lord Cullen, the prosecution lawyer. The 'Narrative', and the events of Christian's case, also bear striking resemblance to events which happened in 1692 at Salem, New England. A version of the case involving Abigail Williams, a twelve-year old girl who experienced violent fits which she blamed on witchcraft, was written by Reverend Deodat Lawson, and published in Boston in 1692. Another version by Cotton Mather followed later. The sentiments expressed by Lawson, affirming the existence of the 'powers of darkness' are also found in the preface to the 'Narrative', which states that this book will serve to glorify God's name. It is possible, therefore, that the 'Narrative' was written, much like Robert Kirk's *Secret Commonwealth*, to prove the existence of God and spirits and to oppose what were seen as the increasingly dangerous forces of scepticism. The presbyterian church in Scotland had faced a number of struggles during the seventeenth century: interference by Charles I, attacks on Covenanting ministers, imposition and later removal of episcopalian church government, and by the late 1680s and 1690s threats from not only sceptics but possible atheists. Many felt that not only was the church beleaguered, but faith in Christianity was being questioned by these ideas. It might be that Christian Shaw's argument with Katherine Campbell was turned into a publicity opportunity for those who felt threatened by those they identified as sadducees – non-believers in spirits.

MARGARET MURDOCH AND MARGARET LAIRD

Two years after the trial in Paisley, two young girls from the same area, claimed that they had been bewitched and demonstrated similar symptoms of demonic possession. Margaret Murdoch's experience was very like Christian's: spasms of rigidity when her limbs could not be moved; vomiting of pins, wool, straw and hair; numerous burns and bruises all over her body. Margaret Laird fell into faints and was unresponsive to people around her. She appeared mute during these episodes, and also experienced convulsions and bodily contortions, reportedly claiming she could see the Devil during these fits.

Like Christian, the two Margarets named and accused a large number of people. Unlike the incident between Christian and Katherine Campbell, there does not seem to have been any personal argument or conflict involving the Margarets which sparked the initial complaint. Sir John Maxwell of Pollok was key to the pursuit of the charges. His father had been the supposed victim of a group of witches and had been involved in their trial in 1677. Maxwell had been an active and enthusiastic commissioner during the Bargarran trial and in 1699 he was appointed Justice Clerk. This seems to have encouraged his involvement and in March 1699 the justice court issued permission to interview witnesses and record their testimonies. Up to twenty people were accused by name, some of whom appear to have had pre-existing, suspicious, reputations amongst the local community. By April a formal indictment was drawn up naming twenty-four people.

Although Maxwell was clearly a significant factor there were other people who were also involved in both cases, particularly James Brisbane, minister at Kilmacolm. Another minister, Neil Gillies, from the Tron in Glasgow, had also been a witness during the Bargarran trial. It seemed as if this trial would progress the same way as the Bargarran one: Maxwell and some of the same ministers were involved and there were two victims to bear witness to the horrific nature of demonic possession. The accused had also confessed to demonic pact and supernatural activities. However, things did not go quite smoothly.

There were numerous delays and by March 1700 the case was dismissed and the accused were freed. The reasons given were that the evidence was not reliable and it would seem, some of those involved in taking down testimonies expressed their doubts: John Anderson, depute-clerk to the Privy Council thought there was little purpose to the trial. Between July and November 1699 there was a lot of disagreement between the local Glasgow / Paisley ministers and the legal authorities in Edinburgh. At one stage the ministers requested that the circuit court trial be cancelled and a local commission granted instead. The justice court refused this as it had been recommended after 1662, by legal experts such as Sir George Mackenzie of Rosehaugh, that all trials should be held before the central justice court as local trials tended to convict more easily.

Undoubtedly the dismissal of this case was regarded as a worrying slight by many of those ministers who were fighting a rearguard action against scepticism, despite their apparent victory at Bargarran. By 1700, belief in the crime of witchcraft was still acceptable for many but the balance had swung in favour of caution – not total rejection – but care over the reliability of evidence and testimony.

Patrick Morton

The last of the demonic possession cases was in 1704 and in Fife, not in the Paisley area. Patrick Morton, a sixteen-year old apprentice blacksmith who also claimed to have experience convulsions and fits. His body became rigid, his back would arch, and he developed a swollen stomach. It also seems that he became weak and emaciated, although he stopped eating which probably did not help his symptoms. He also complained of being punched and pricked all over his body. The symptoms were very similar to Christian and to the two Margarets, although like Christian's case there seems to have been an initial dispute between Patrick and one of the accused, Beatrix Laing.

It seems that Beatrix Laing, who was the wife of a local tailor, had requested Patrick to make her some nails, a request that he had refused. It may be that she muttered something which expressed her annoyance, she already had a bit of a reputation amongst the local population as she had been refused communion and was regarded as a woman of 'ill fame'. Whatever the case, Patrick interpreted this as a curse and when he began to complain of strange symptoms and bewitching he identified Beatrix as a likely source. Patrick Cowper, who was the local minister, had read the account of Christian Shaw's sufferings and it would seem quite possible that this may have had some influence on the symptoms Patrick experienced, or claimed to experience.

The hunt spread rapidly and seven others were named by Beartrix, although she later retracted these: Janet Cornfoot or Corphat, Nicolas Lawson, Janet Horseburgh, Isobel Adam and Thomas Brown and Lilias Wallace were named as accomplices. Another woman, Margaret Jack, was also implicated but like Brown, Horseburgh and Wallace, she did not confess.

Patrick made his accusations and the minister and bailies of Pittenweem imprisoned the seven in

Pittenweem Tolbooth, the accused were imprisoned here.

the tolbooth and questioned and examined them. Laing, Cornfoot, Lawson, and Adam all confessed to renunciation of their baptism, making a demonic pact and attending meetings. They were pricked – examined for the Devil's mark – and deprived of sleep in order to encourage their confessions. Beartrix later appealed to the Privy Council claiming that because she would not confess she had been tortured by being kept awake for five days and nights and was continually pricked on the shoulders, back and thighs. In June the kirk session, and then the presbytery of St Andrews, examined the accused and witnesses and later the burgh council of Pittenweem petitioned the Privy Council for a commission. Indeed they cited the precedent of the Bargarran case in their petition, probably on the advice of Cowper.

Friends of the accused had petitioned to have them released, but they were ordered to stand trial in Edinburgh, where they were examined in November 1704, in front of the Lord Advocate. They were all subsequently released and Patrick Morton was declared a liar. There is some evidence that the accused were ordered to pay a fine of £8 Scots for their freedom, which they appeared to have paid. Thomas Brown had died earlier, of starvation, when imprisoned in the tolbooth at Pittenweem (the building survives although some have claimed that it is haunted, the activity perhaps linked to this episode). The others, apart from Janet Cornfoot, survived the accusation and examination, although Beartrix wrote to the Privy Council asking for protection and detailing her ill treatment at the hands of the townspeople. Protection was granted in May 1705 and she moved to St Andrews.

Despite the adjudication of the lord advocate, the community of Pittenweem, encouraged by Patrick Cowper, the minister, did not accept the verdict. When Janet had fled to Leuchars, (about twelve miles or so from Pittenweem) she was sent back by the minister, and in January 1705 she was set upon by the villagers of Pittenweem, apparently in an attempt to make her confess – which she refused to do. She was dragged through the streets, suspended from ropes tied between a boat and the shore and stoned. They then cut her down and brought her back on land where they laid a heavy wooden door on top of her and crushed her to death by piling stones on top of the door and then driving a cart over her. The poor woman had refused to confess and the mob murdered her.

The bailies eventually reported the incident to the Privy Council in February and claimed that several of those involved had been imprisoned but that Cowper had released them. Patrick Morton had been identified as an impostor but he was not punished.

It was a shameful episode that demonstrated the dangers of mob violence: as individuals people can behave reasonably, but this self control is often lost in a crowd or mob, which often act quite unreasonably. The ordinary townsfolk of Pittenweem seemed to have had concerns about Beatrix Laing, as she already had a bad reputation, but there seems to be no evidence of previous concerns about the others. So was this an example of a town panicking, feeling justified fear, or were they deliberately stirred up into a frenzy? If the latter is the case, who stirred up emotions? Patrick was a cheat and liar, but why would he want to create a moral panic in an east-coast fishing village? Perhaps he was as suggestible as the other three, Christian and the two Margarets. How much did the minister Patrick Cowper influence events and actions? It does seem likely that he encouraged Patrick in his claims about being bewitched, he was aware of the details of the Bargarran case, he arranged for those involved in the lynch mob to be released from custody, and he did little to intervene to prevent an extra-judicial execution. It would seem that Cowper was of the same opinion as the authors of the 'Narrative', and may have believed that the threat from demonic spirits was a real and present one and that the afflictions experienced by these young people would demonstrate to any doubters the reality of these evil spirits.

In a written account of the Pittenweem case, 'A True and Full Relation of the Witches at Pittenweem', which was published in Edinburgh in 1704-05, the author claimed that Morton's experience would be used for the same purpose as Christian's, to prove the existence of good and evil spirits. It does seem unfortunate, to us, that these seventeenth-century Scottish ministers felt that in order to prove the existence of God they had to prove the existence of evil, and to do so they felt justified in manipulating young people, who may have been vulnerable, which then resulted in the execution of seven people, the starving to death of another man and the horrific murder of Janet Cornfoot by her own community.

Janet Horne
1722 or 1727

Most accounts of witch trials in Scotland mention
that the last execution apparently took place in
Dornoch, Sutherland, although the whole episode
is quite poorly recorded and the details are disputed:
the date of the execution has been recorded as either
1722 or 1727 and even the names of the women are
uncertain.

There is a small stone in Dornoch inscribed
with the date 1722, said to mark the place where
traditionally, a Janet Horne was executed for
witchcraft. It is claimed that she was accused of
several practices including bizarrely turning her
daughter into a pony so she could ride her to
meetings with the Devil. Another account mentions
that she was dragged through the streets of the town
before being burned in a barrel of tar.

There are no surviving contemporary records,
such as local kirk session or presbytery minutes, or
applications for commissions, to provide any reliable
first-hand primary evidence. Therefore a lot of what
is claimed about this case is derived from much later
accounts based on hearsay, second-hand accounts,
and oral tradition.

One of the first documentary reports about
Janet came from Captain Edmund Burt, who was
employed to work on the construction of roads in
the north of Scotland during the 1720s and 1730s –

sometime after the Jacobite Rising of 1715. He was somewhat surprised to note that in the Highlands of Scotland belief about witches was still quite widespread. His account has two women from Loth in Sutherland (about twenty miles from Dornoch), an unnamed mother and daughter, who were tried for witchcraft and condemned to death. The younger woman escaped, but the older woman was burned in a 'pitch barrel at Dornoch' in 1727.

Burt's account was published in 1754, well after the supposed event, and it is not clear if Burt witnessed it or if he simply relied on hearsay evidence. The 1727 date appears to be supported by an account by James Fraser of Alness who mentioned an anonymous case from Loth in 1727 and Thomas Pennant, who toured Scotland in 1769, recorded that he had heard an account of what were said to be the last executions in 1727. A later version in Sinclair's *Statistical Account* of the 1790s stated somewhat vaguely that between 1717 and 1730 the last 'unhappy woman' was executed for witchcraft at Dornoch.

In 1819 another version by Charles Kirkpatrick Sharpe dated the execution to 1722, and provided further details about the case including a description of the mother riding her daughter, who was transformed into a pony and shod by the Devil. It was this Devilish procedure that made the daughter lame thereafter. It is in Sharpe's account that the description of the supposedly elderly Janet warming herself by the fire before being burnt first appeared. This later account was given credibility by Sir Walter

Scott, who was a supporter of the much maligned Countess of Sutherland. The countess told Scott about the execution, as it related to her family's estates, and her account mentioned that the daughter had burnt her hands when she was a child and had suffered from scarring which caused her hands to look twisted and contracted. According to the countess, it was popularly believed that the mother had caused the accident by witchcraft. Although to confuse the matter further – and to add weight to a completely natural physical abnormality – it was also claimed by the countess that the grandson of the daughter still lived locally (in the early nineteenth century) and that all subsequent generations of the family had the same sort of anomaly.

It is not clear when the woman was given the name Janet or Jenny Horne; all versions until the twentieth century made no reference to her name. It may well be that the name is fictitious as Jenny Horne is the north-east term for a witch.

Although the subject of a play by Rona Munro, *The Last Witch*, there is so much that is either unknown or inaccurate that it is almost impossible to even claim that this was the last execution in Scotland. Even if she was apocryphal, however, Janet or Jenny can still be memorialised as a representation of the many other, named, women and men who were executed in earlier years.

The event is said to be commemorated in more than just literature. For the ghost of Janet Horne is reputed seen sometimes at the stone, being consumed by spectral flames in a barrel of pitch.